MW00929284

NOTEBOOK

RULED PAPER

THIS BOOK BELONGS TO:

authored by: Marcel Doll, Hammerschbüchel 10, 53797 Lohmar, Germany

Made in the USA
Monee, IL
25 February 2022

91807037R00069